MAD SCIENTISTS

IN FACT
AND
FICTION

MAD SCIENTISTS

IN FACT
AND
FICTION

BY MELVIN BERGER

FRANKLIN WATTS
NEW YORK | LONDON | TORONTO | SYDNEY | 1980

The photograph opposite the title page is from the film *Murders in the Rue Morgue*. The photograph opposite p. 55 is of a creature from the film *The Island of Dr. Moreau*. The photograph opposite p. 72 is of Dr. Gogol from the film *Mad Love*.

Photographs courtesy of Universal Studios: opp. title page, pp. 4 (top), 47, 48, 68, 69, 76, 77, 80, 81; New York Public Library Picture Collection: pp. 3 (both), 10 (both), 14 (middle), 24 (both), 28, 29, 31 (all), 38; 20th Century-Fox: pp. 4 (bottom), 51 (bottom); Columbia Pictures: p. 5; College of Philadelphia: p. 14 (top); NASA: p. 32; from the book *Journey Underground* (1741): p. 35 (bottom); from the 1831 edition of the novel *Frankenstein*: p. 44; Warner Brothers: pp. 51 (top), 65; American International: pp. 52, 53, 54, 70; Paramount Pictures: pp. 57, 78; from the 1931 edition of the novel *The Man Who Evolved*: p. 58; MGM: pp. 62, 63, 66, 72; National: p. 82.

Library of Congress Cataloging in Publication Data

Berger, Melvin.
Mad scientists in fact and fiction.

Bibliography: p.
Includes index.
SUMMARY: Discusses those scientists, real and fictional, who have espoused unusual theories, often in conjunction with bizarre experiments.
1. Scientists—Juvenile literature.
[1. Scientists] I. Title.
Q163.B499   509.2′2   80–13718
ISBN 0–531–04153–0

CONTENTS

MAD SCIENTISTS IN FICTION

MAD SCIENTISTS

IN FACT
AND
FICTION

CHAPTER 1

INTRODUCTION

A man comes into the office of Dr. Albert Abrams in San Francisco. He complains of pains in his stomach.

"Your vibrations are out of harmony," says Dr. Abrams. "That is the cause of almost all disease."

The doctor asks his assistant to come into the room. He attaches a wire from a series of connected electrical machines to the assistant's forehead. Then he draws a drop of blood from the patient's finger and places it into one of the machines.

"My machine is picking up your vibrations from the blood sample. It is transmitting them to my healthy assistant over there."

The uncomfortable man anxiously awaits the doctor's diagnosis.

"Just as I suspected," Dr. Abrams finally says. "Your liver is off by 5 volts."

The doctor moves some other machines over to the patient.

[1]

"We'll apply the correct vibrations to your liver, and you'll be fine by tomorrow."

"Thank you, thank you, Doctor," the patient murmurs as Dr. Abrams holds a wire coil against his stomach. "I feel better already."

A doctor is bent over the operating table in his large, dimly lit laboratory. On the table lies the inert, heavily bandaged figure of a man. He is made up of body parts stolen from corpses.

Outside a terrible storm is raging. Blinding streaks of lightning illuminate the laboratory. The doctor watches as a tremendous bolt strikes the unmoving figure.

Very slowly the figure comes to life. The hand that was hanging over the side of the table begins to stir. Within moments the man-made creature rises from the table.

"It's alive, it's alive!" Dr. Frankenstein shrieks.

Both of these stories are about mad scientists—one in fact, one in fiction.

Dr. Abrams was a mad scientist in fact. He was a medical quack. Doctors like him treat their patients with useless or even dangerous electrical machines, magnetic forces, magic wands, or worthless drugs. They promise instant cures for all sorts of diseases.

There are also mad scientists in fact who claim to have special knowledge about the workings of nature. They search for formulas that will accomplish changes other scientists believe to be impossible, such as turning lead into gold or old age into youth. Their methods often have no logic or system. Their conclusions are rarely based on reason. And the results of their experiments can almost never be duplicated.

There are some mad scientists in fact who talk about collisions with comets or visitors from outer space. Others insist, in spite of the evidence, that the earth is flat or that they can build a machine that will run forever on almost no fuel. And this is only a sampling of the mad scientists of fact.

Then there are the mad scientists of fiction. Those like Dr. Frankenstein tamper in their laboratories with nature's deepest secrets. Often their purpose is to create live beings using artificial methods. The beings created this way are usually monsters who com-

Some mad
scientists in
fact treated
their patients
with useless
electrical
machines.

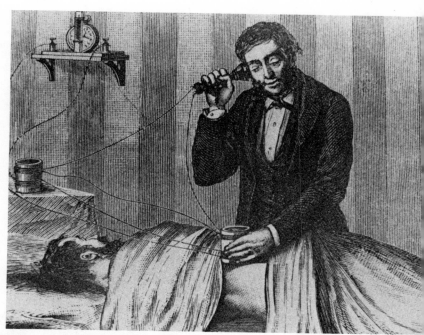

Others worked
for years to
change lead
into gold.

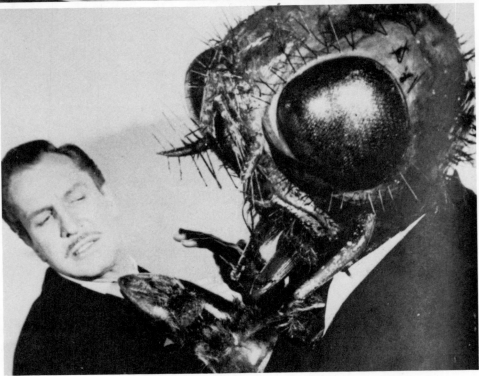

Left: some mad scientists of fiction tamper in their laboratories with nature's deepest secrets. Above: these fictional mad scientists are trying to record people's thoughts.

mit acts of violence. Almost always they end up killing or bringing death upon the scientists who gave them life.

Another group of fictional mad scientists work to alter natural processes. They may do experiments with drugs or rays that turn ordinary people into murderers or automatons.

Though they are not necessarily insane, the mad scientists of fact and fiction hold unorthodox, often bizarre, views. Their experiments do little to increase real scientific knowledge. Many of these scientists refuse to accept the laws of the universe. Their theories usually do not lead anywhere. A majority of these scientists are more interested in power and personal gain than in contributing to the common good.

Yet the mad scientist, real or fictional, has always been a very popular character. In the following pages you will meet some of the best known, most typical, and strangest mad scientists of fact and fiction. Some are amusing. Many are frightening. But all are fascinating.

MAD SCIENTISTS

IN FACT

CHAPTER 2

DAFFY DOCTORS
MEDICAL MADNESS

Franz Anton Mesmer was perhaps the greatest medical fraud, or quack, of all time, even though he was able to cure some people and some aspects of his work have been incorporated into modern medicine. So famous were Mesmer's activities that his name has become part of the English language in the word *mesmerize,* which means to hypnotize or put someone into a trance.

Mesmer was born in Austria in 1734 and received his medical degree from the University of Vienna. Early in his career, Dr. Mesmer became familiar with the work of several doctors, including the sixteenth-century Swiss physician and alchemist, Paracelsus, and a seventeenth-century German professor of medicine, Sebastian Wirdig, both of whom advocated the use of magnetism to treat human disease. Paracelsus used a magnetic stone to treat certain diseases. Wirdig, who taught at the University of Rostok, treated his patients by changing their magnetic field.

Dr. Franz
Anton Mesmer
was one
of the best
known of all
medical quacks.

In Dr. Mesmer's
treatment room
the patients sat
around the *baquet*
to allow the
magnetism to
flow through
their bodies.

But it was the work of a contemporary, a Jesuit priest named Maximilian Hell, that had the greatest influence on Mesmer's ideas concerning magnetism. Hell, who taught astronomy at the University of Vienna, was attempting to cure various diseases by holding iron plates against the affected parts of the body.

Mesmer came to believe that every person's body contains an invisible magnetic fluid, creating an animal magnetism different from the magnetism that attracts metals. This fluid, Mesmer claimed, could flow in and out of bodies, could be reflected by mirrors, and could be stored in batteries. It was problems in the flow of the fluid that caused sickness.

Mesmer believed that his own body contained an especially great amount of the fluid, which he could use to cure others. One of his patients, a young woman, suffered from dizziness and rushes of blood to her head. Mesmer attempted to bathe the woman in his magnetism by moving his hands over her. This put her into a trance and apparently freed her from the symptoms of her disease for hours after each treatment. On the basis of these few symptom-free hours Mesmer claimed he had cured the woman. Mesmer also claimed to cure a young woman who was blind and suffered from convulsions. But this claim was much disputed by other doctors in Vienna.

Realizing that his reputation was in danger, Mesmer moved to Paris in 1778. There he set up a large and luxurious treatment room. Heavy draperies covered the windows, and there were thick carpets on the floor. The semi-dark room was filled with the scent of perfume, and a small orchestra played behind a screen.

In the middle of the room was a *baquet,* a large oval tub about 1 foot (.3 m) deep and 4 feet (1.2 m) long. The *baquet* held water that had been sprinkled with iron filings (for their magnetic qualities) and ground glass. Magnetized water in bottles floated in the bath. A big iron lid, with a number of iron rods poking up through it, covered the *baquet.*

The patients, up to thirty at a time, sat around the tub grasping the rods, in order to allow the magnetism to flow through their bodies. After a while, several of Mesmer's assistants would come in. These handsome young men would stare into the patients' eyes as they massaged the painful or affected parts. The patients, who were mostly women, either cried, laughed, or passed out.

Eventually Dr. Mesmer, wearing a flowing purple silk robe and carrying a white iron wand, would enter. He'd pass among the patients, reviving them. Very gently he'd touch his wand to the diseased area to allow his own powerful magnetism to flow in. At the end of the treatment, a certain number of people would always insist that they had been cured.

Great arguments raged over Mesmer. Thomas Jefferson called him a maniac. But Lafayette, the renowned French general and statesman, often went to Mesmer for treatments. Most doctors, though, regarded him with suspicion.

In 1784, King Louis XVI formed a commission to investigate Mesmer. It included the chemist Antoine Lavoisier and Benjamin Franklin, known as widely at the time for his experiments with electricity as for his political achievements.

The commission conducted many tests of Mesmer's treatment methods. In one test, a mesmerist brought his hand near a woman he was treating, and she described herself as feeling warm. Then she was blindfolded, and although the doctor repeated the same movement, she reported feeling nothing. In the third trial she was again blindfolded, and although the mesmerist did not approach her, she said she felt his warmth.

In another test, a mesmerist treated seven patients in Benjamin Franklin's Paris home. Four felt nothing when the magnetism was applied. Three reported some pain. None was cured.

In September 1784, the commission concluded that there was no such thing as animal magnetism or magnetic fluid. They attributed Mesmer's cures to an "excitement of the imagination." Today we call this hypnotic suggestion. Hypnotism is still used in treating diseases for which there are no known organic causes. But it cannot, as far as we know, bring about a cure unless the illness is a symptom of a psychological problem.

Around this same time, a physician in the United States was becoming known for his invention of Metallic Tractors. Dr. Elisha Perkins, a surgeon of Norwich, Connecticut, noticed that when his metal surgical instruments touched a patient's muscle, the muscle contracted. From this observation, he evolved a theory that holding metal rods to the body could cure everything from aches and pains to paralysis.

In 1796 Perkins' Metallic Tractors became the first medical item to be patented under the Constitution. They were two metal rods, about 3 inches (7.6 cm) long, pointed at one end and rounded at the other. According to Perkins, one rod contained gold and the other platinum. (Perkins' critics insisted the two rods were really just brass and iron.)

Perkins' treatments could not be simpler. The doctor drew the Metallic Tractors in one direction or another over the affected area, depending on the location and type of disease. The correct movement was considered most important; the wrong direction could be fatal.

Soon after devising his rods, Perkins went to Philadelphia, the seat of the newly formed United States government, to demonstrate his invention. Some of the highest officials there were very impressed with what they saw. George Washington was among those who purchased Perkins' rods.

Though Perkins was able to fool members of the general public, most doctors were not impressed. In fact, two of them made rods of wood, painted them to look like metal, tested them on their own patients, and got the same results—or lack of results—as Perkins. The Connecticut Medical Society decided to drop Dr. Perkins from its membership.

In 1799, when a serious yellow fever epidemic struck New York City, Dr. Perkins came forward with a cure for the disease. It consisted of a solution of salt in vinegar. Sad to say, Perkins himself died of the disease on September 6, 1799.

His son, Benjamin Douglas Perkins, also a doctor, carried forward his father's work in Britain. He continued to sell the tractors and he created the Perkins Institute and Dispensary to do further research on the rods. In time, though, British doctors became convinced that the tractors had no special healing power, and the young Dr. Perkins was laughed out of the country. The Metallic Tractors soon faded from the medical scene.

While magnetic treatments were disappearing at the start of the nineteenth century, another approach to medicine, called homeopathy, was emerging. The founder of homeopathy was Samuel Frederick Christian Hahnemann, born in Meissen, Germany, in 1755. Hahnemann received his degree in medicine from the University of Erlangen.

Early in his career Hahnemann found that if he took some cinchona bark extract, a drug used in the treatment of malaria, it chilled his hands and feet, caused palpitations of his heart, a

Dr. Perkins' Metallic Tractors were two metal rods about 3 inches (7.6 cm) long. Treatment with Dr. Perkins' rods was frequently the subject of cartoons.

Right: Dr. Samuel Frederick Christian Hahnemann, born in 1755, was the founder of homeopathy.

throbbing head, flushed cheeks, and a fever. These are the symptoms of malaria itself. From this Hahnemann reasoned that he could cure many diseases by prescribing small doses of drugs that produced the same symptoms as the diseases themselves.

Some three thousand homeopathic drugs have been discovered over the years since Hahnemann. Among them are *lachryma filia* (a young girl's tears), *mephitis* (skunk secretion), *cimex lectularius* (crushed live bedbugs), powdered coal, and powdered oyster shells. Since Hahnemann believed that the less of the drug used, the greater its "spiritual" effect, the doses were seldom large enough to cause any change in the patient's condition.

In time, homeopathy became widely accepted in both Britain and the United States. Ralph Waldo Emerson and William Cullen Bryant were two prominent Americans who were ardent believers in homeopathy. The British royal family appointed a homeopath as their official physician. By 1900 there were twenty-two homeopathic colleges in the United States. With the development of modern medicine, however, the popularity of homeopathy began to wane, though it has still not disappeared altogether.

Dr. Albert Abrams was a well-trained, highly respected physician. Born in San Francisco in 1863, he earned his medical degree at the University of Heidelberg in Germany and did postgraduate study at the universities of Berlin, Vienna, London, and Paris.

As a young man of twenty-seven, Dr. Abrams returned to San Francisco, where he was appointed to the staff of the Cooper Medical College. In 1910, he published his first book, in which he described a method of diagnosing illness by tapping on the patient's spine. Six years later he stated that diseases appear when the electrons (atomic particles) in a particular organ are vibrating out of harmony. Treatment consisted of restoring the normal rate of vibration.

To help with his diagnoses, Abrams invented several electrical machines. Eventually he evolved an entire medical procedure that he called the Electronic Reactions of Abrams (ERA).

Abrams would take a few drops of blood from the patient while the patient faced west. He'd then place the blood on a piece of filter paper and insert it into the first of his machines, the Dynamizer. The Dynamizer was connected to three other machines, the Rheostatic Dynamizer, the Vibratory Rate Rheostat, and the Measuring Rheostat. (A rheostat is a simple device that controls the flow of electrical current by changing the resistance in the circuit.)

A healthy subject, stripped to the waist and facing west in a dimly lit room, would stand near the final machine, the Measuring Rheostat, with an electrode from the machine attached to his or her forehead. Dr. Abrams claimed that the machine was able to pick up the vibrations of the patient's blood and transmit them to the healthy subject. By then tapping the healthy subject's abdomen, Abrams said he could diagnose the patient's disease. He said that he could learn a person's sex and religion the same way!

The follow-up treatment involved another of Dr. Abrams' machines, the Oscilloclast. The doctor would adjust the machine's speed and then apply the vibrations to the patient to destroy the disease. By 1923, about 3,500 practitioners were using Abrams' methods. His factory had produced over 4,000 ERA machines.

Many thousands of people were willing to pay for diagnosis and treatment by Dr. Abrams and his followers. But there were skeptics as well.

One doctor drew some blood from a healthy male guinea pig and sent it to an ERA practitioner in New Mexico. He said it was from a patient of his and that he wanted a diagnosis. The reply was that the patient suffered from cancer in the amount of 5 ohms (an ohm is a unit of electrical resistance) and from a sinus infection. Another doctor in Michigan sent Dr. Abrams a sample of rooster blood. Abrams wrote back that the patient was suffering from malaria, cancer, diabetes, and two different kinds of venereal disease!

Dr. Abrams died in 1923, leaving an estate of $2 million. Despite strict instructions never to open the machines, some brave souls took a look inside. They found a number of electrical components, rheostats, ohmmeters, and condensers, all wired together in an apparently random and meaningless way.

From the rituals and chants of witch doctors to the most advanced treatments by modern physicians, medicine has had more than its share of odd, rebellious, or dishonest practitioners. At best, these medical quacks cure by faith or heal by the power of suggestion. At worst, they administer remedies that not only fail to cure but may even cause harm. Yet so long as there are people who seek miracle cures, there will be doctors of questionable integrity around ready to try to provide them.

CHAPTER 3

CRAZY CHEMISTS
THE ALCHEMISTS

The first of the known alchemists was Zosimos, who lived in ancient Greece about 1,600 years ago. He wrote that all metals are living things. Only two, silver and gold, are in good health. All the others are ailing.

According to Zosimos, the alchemist's job was to kill the sick metal and bring it back to life as one of the valuable healthy metals. The directions Zosimos gave for accomplishing this, however, were so deliberately vague and hard to understand—Zosimos didn't want anyone to learn his secrets—that no one has ever been able to follow them successfully.

The basic aim of all alchemy was to bring about changes, or transmutations. The transmutations were sought by chemical means but did not utilize the logic or systematic approach of the science of chemistry. The transmutation of metals, such as lead, iron, and mercury into silver and gold, was one of the most important activities of the alchemists. But they also worked to bring about other desir-

Nicolas Flamel (right), born in 1330, was the most famous of the early alchemists. The illustration below is from a book by Flamel.

able changes, such as illness into good health and old age into youth.

Alchemy spread to western Europe during the Middle Ages. The French-born Nicolas Flamel (1330–1418) was one of the most famous of the early alchemists. He tried to find the philosopher's stone, a magical substance thought to make transmutations possible because it contained the spirit of life.

Before turning to alchemy, Flamel had a very successful career as a public scribe—writing letters, copying books, and teaching the children of the well-to-do. In 1357, though, he had a dream that changed the direction of his life. In the dream an angel brought him a book entitled *The Book of Abraham the Jew*. The book was bound in copper, with pages made of thin sheets of tree bark. The angel told Flamel that one day he would understand the book's meaning. When Flamel reached for the book in his dream, though, both book and angel disappeared.

A few days later, Flamel came across the very book he had dreamed about. He bought it and took it home. With his wife, Pernella, Flamel went through "a thousand bungling trials" to find the philosopher's stone.

After twenty years of effort, Flamel finally claimed he had found it. It was a brilliant white powder. Flamel said that by applying this powder, called an elixir, to lead, he could produce pure silver. Months later, "while carefully minding every word in the book," Flamel found another elixir, red and foul-smelling. This elixir, he said, could change mercury into gold.

Flamel and his wife devoted the rest of their lives to religion and good works. They donated the money for the building of seven churches and fourteen hospitals. The question of where the money came from has never been answered.

Another unanswered question involves the explosion that destroyed Flamel's house right after he died. Some said the house exploded because the alchemist had made a pact with the devil. But there was also talk that would-be robbers had torn the house apart while frantically searching for Flamel's magical elixirs.

All that is known for sure is that Nicolas Flamel's writings on alchemy remained popular until the eighteenth century. By then Europe had changed, and many European countries had begun to be ruled by powerful kings. The alchemists dropped their quest for the elixirs of life and began to spend all their time trying to produce gold for the power-hungry kings and other nobles.

The alchemists did not, of course, succeed. Many were thrown into prison and tortured. But some, like Giuseppe Balsamo, became rich and famous.

Balsamo was born in Palermo, Sicily, in 1743. Having been caught stealing from a local monastery, the young Balsamo left Palermo for the island of Malta, where he first studied alchemy.

Several years of adventure followed, during which time Balsamo got married and also served a jail sentence for forgery. In 1772 he arrived in London. British investors gave Balsamo large sums of money in exchange for his promise to provide them with silver, gold, and cure-all medicines. When the investors became impatient with Balsamo's endless delays, he was again imprisoned.

Balsamo next appeared in Paris, where he put on an amazing display, changing mercury into gold. The audience, of course, did not see Balsamo substituting real gold, which he had hidden, for the mercury. Now it was the Parisians who gave him great amounts of money for the gold he would produce for them. But again Balsamo failed to come up with any gold, and so, facing jail still another time, he fled.

Although he had yet to produce a true transmutation of any kind, Balsamo's fame continued to grow. He moved from city to city, making and selling elixirs to cure disease, lengthen life, improve appearance, and, most important of all, create gold. Among his products were "Egyptian Wine," which proved to be nothing more than cheap French wine with spices added, and "Refreshing Pills," made up mostly of lettuce!

Balsamo prospered. He lived in grand style, with servants and secretaries, and gave every sign of having unlimited funds. He became an international celebrity. A likeness of his face appeared on plates, jewelry, fans, snuff boxes, and kerchiefs. Paintings and busts of him were displayed in many of the better homes.

Balsamo reached the height of his fame in Paris in 1785. By then he had given himself a title, Count Cagliostro, and as Cagliostro he became involved in a major scandal involving a diamond necklace. After being sentenced to prison he was freed but told to leave France. Some five thousand of his followers accompanied him to the port and knelt on the shore as his ship departed.

**Count Cagliostro, born Giuseppe Balsamo,
became rich and well established as an alchemist.**

Misfortune followed Cagliostro from that point on. Eventually he was sentenced to death by the Inquisition for making anti-Catholic statements. In 1791, the Pope commuted the sentence to life imprisonment, but Cagliostro died in jail four years later.

By the time of Cagliostro's death, almost no one believed in transmutation or alchemy. But it remained for a nineteenth-century British physician and alchemist to bring the practice to a final close.

Early in the century, Dr. James Price aroused a good deal of interest when he published a pamphlet giving a formula for the transmutation of metals. He decided to give a public demonstration of his ideas.

The demonstration was well attended. Price showed his audience a white powder that he had prepared and added to it fifty times its weight in mercury plus some borax and nitre. He then heated the mixture, stirring it with a special iron rod. When it cooled, Price amazed the distinguished audience with the resulting metal. It was pure silver.

Next Price mixed together a red powder and sixty times its weight in mercury. This time he produced pure gold. Both metals were later tested and pronounced to be absolutely pure.

So convincing was this demonstration that Price was invited to repeat his performance before the scientists of the Royal Society. The doctor kept postponing his appearance. Finally, when he could put it off no longer, he invited the group to his home outside of London. As soon as everyone was assembled, Price entered the room. Then, in full view of the committee, he swallowed a lethal dose of poison.

A court of inquiry investigated his death. Was Price an alchemist, an impostor, or was he insane? The coroner concluded that Dr. Price was indeed mad.

We now know that the alchemists had no chance for success. Elements can be combined by chemical means to form compounds such as water. Compounds can also be split apart by chemical means. But there is no chemical means of changing any element, including lead or mercury, into another element, such as silver or gold.

The only way that elements can actually be changed is by nuclear reactions. Nuclear fission can split atoms apart; nuclear fusion can join atoms together. But no nuclear reaction has thus far been able to produce a valuable metal.

CHAPTER 4

ASTOUNDING ASTRONOMERS
NEW EXPLANATIONS
FOR PAST EVENTS

According to Dr. Immanuel Velikovsky, there was a gigantic explosion on the planet Jupiter about 3,500 years ago. An immense comet was torn out of the planet and was sent hurtling out into the solar system. As this comet passed near earth it caused a number of events to occur that are described in the Bible and other ancient writings.

Some material from the comet fell to earth in the river Nile, turning the water red. Flies and vermin that were living on the comet fell to earth and swarmed over Egypt. The passing comet raised the temperature on earth so high that frogs in large numbers were born.

Other results of the near miss were severe earthquakes in Egypt and a vast tidal wave in the Red Sea that caused the waters to part. Some of the comet's tail fell to earth and was used as food by the people of Israel in their flight from Egypt. Later the same comet again passed quite close to the earth. This time it stopped the earth in its rotation, leaving the planet immobile in space for a whole day

In the Bible, Moses parts the Red Sea (above) and
Joshua commands the sun to stand still (below).
Velikovsky's explanations for these events is
that a comet passed very close to earth.

and thus making it appear, as described in the Biblical tale of Joshua, that the sun had been commanded to stand still. Finally, the comet fell into orbit as the planet Venus.

Immanuel Velikovsky, author of these ideas, was born in Russia in 1895. In addition to receiving a doctor of medicine degree from the University of Moscow, Velikovsky studied natural science at the University of Edinburgh, biology at the University of Berlin, and psychoanalysis at the University of Vienna. He came to the United States in 1939 and lived there until his death in 1979.

In his 1950 book, *Worlds in Collision,* Velikovsky first summarized his startling theories connecting Biblical and other legendary accounts of events with natural events occurring at around the same time.

Because of Velikovsky's excellent training in science and his many convincing arguments, large numbers of people accepted his views. In the early 1970s, a group in Portland, Oregon, calling itself the Student Academic Freedom Forum, started a journal that presented Velikovsky's arguments and ideas.

Still, many scientists refused to accept what Velikovsky was saying. In 1974, at the annual meeting of the American Association for the Advancement of Science, five leading scientists presented arguments in opposition to Velikovsky's theories.

The scientists said, for instance, that there was no evidence that a comet had ever, in the history of our solar system, been ejected from a planet. Furthermore, the energy required to remove a mass the size of Venus would have generated so much heat that it would have completely melted Jupiter. In addition, if Venus came from Jupiter, then both bodies should be made of the same materials. Yet Jupiter consists mostly of hydrogen and helium gases, while Venus is composed of rock and metal, like earth. Finally, one scientist claimed that the odds for the five near collisions that Velikovsky said took place between 1500 and 500 B.C. are one hundred billion trillion to one—which most scientists call an impossibility.

As to the flies and vermin that supposedly fell to earth from the comet, the scientists pointed out that recent spaceshots have proven that no such life forms exist on either Venus or Jupiter. Other spaceshots have shown that no living thing could survive a trip through space or a fall through the earth's atmosphere without protection. Nor has research on comets and their tails revealed any substance that could turn water red or be eaten by humans.

[25]

Velikovsky's argument for the earth's standing still was also shown to be unsound. Suppose the rapidly spinning earth *were* suddenly stopped. Every object and person would be flung off into space at a speed of thousands of miles an hour. Also, the energy needed to stop the earth's rotation would generate so much heat that the oceans would be set boiling.

The exodus of the Jews from Egypt that Velikovsky refers to is believed to have taken place around 1500 B.C. Just about that time there was an immense volcanic eruption on the island of Thera in the Aegean Sea, 500 miles (800 km) north of Egypt. It is possible that the force of that explosion caused an earthquake in Egypt and sent a tidal wave through the Red Sea, making it appear as though the waters had actually parted. The dust thrown up by a big volcano could have caused the three days of darkness in Egypt that the Bible mentions. And the aftereffects of the volcano might have led to a big increase in the number of flies, vermin, and frogs.

All of Velikovsky's arguments are based on the belief that the earth had a number of near misses with other celestial bodies. While there may have been a few such near misses in the billions of years of earth's history, there is no evidence of any near miss within the last few thousand years.

Reports of UFOs (Unidentified Flying Objects) and spaceships landing on earth inspired Erich von Däniken's scientific speculations. In his 1968 book, *Chariots of the Gods?,* von Däniken put forth the idea that visitors from outer space came to earth in the distant past, before 500 B.C. These astronauts, von Däniken said, came from civilizations much more advanced than ours and left evidence of their visits to earth.

Von Däniken was born in Switzerland in 1935. He developed an early interest in history and archeology. After high school he worked as a hotel manager in Davos, Switzerland. Through studying and reading widely, von Däniken became a self-taught expert on our ancient past. He also journeyed around the world and visited nearly all the important archeological sites.

Many scientists believe that there may indeed be intelligent beings elsewhere in the universe, some of whom are probably more advanced and highly developed than we are. But these same scientists seriously question von Däniken's so-called "proof" of visits from ancient astronauts.

[26]

Take the stone carving found in Chiapes, Mexico, made by the Mayan Indians around 683 A.D. Von Däniken claims the carving commemorates a visit by someone from another planet. In it he sees an astronaut, wearing a spacesuit, a helmet, and an oxygen mask, seated in a rocket and adjusting the controls with his hands while his feet are operating foot pedals. On the front of the spaceship, according to von Däniken, are large magnets to repel particles that might damage the craft during flight. Behind the astronaut is a nuclear fusion reactor that supplies the power.

Archeologists have an entirely different understanding of the carving. From the writing on the stone they have learned that the figure is a certain King Pacal, who lived from 603 to 683. The ruler is wearing a typical Mayan outfit, which includes a headpiece covering part of the face and jewelry around the neck, ankles, and wrists.

Pacal is seated on a highly decorated cross that represents a corn plant, the Mayan symbol of rebirth. This cross often appears on carvings of dead rulers or heroes. What von Däniken calls the control panel is, according to archeologists, a two-headed serpent that is draped over the cross bar. At the front end is not a magnet but a *quetzal,* a bird sacred to the Mayans and Aztecs. And the figure is not sitting in front of a nuclear reactor but before a carving of his royal symbol.

Ever since the tiny Pacific land called Easter Island was discovered in 1722, people have wondered about the hundreds of massive statues found there. The statues are made out of volcanic rock and some weigh as much as 50 tons (46 m.t.).

According to von Däniken, the statues were carved by a group of astronauts who landed on the island in the distant past and carved the statues with tools that they brought with them. When they returned to their home planet, von Däniken says, they left hundreds of the statues unfinished.

Most archeologists today believe that the statues were carved by early inhabitants of the island. Their descendants, the modern-day residents of the island, have actually demonstrated for scientists the carving methods that were probably used. The scientists estimate that it took two teams of six men one year to finish a medium-sized statue.

The islanders have also shown how groups of men using wooden sleds could have moved the huge stone carvings and then stood

Left: Von Däniken writes that the
Chiapes carving shows an ancient
astronaut. The more common belief
is that it is a Mayan king. **Above:**
the massive statues on Easter Island
weigh up to 50 tons (46 m.t.) each.

them in place using long wooden poles as levers. The scientists estimate that it would take twelve men about eighteen days to move and erect one statue. The reason for the half-finished statues, say the scientists, was that in 1680 a civil war broke out on the island and all work stopped, never to start again.

Astronauts also built the Egyptian pyramids, claims von Däniken. He says that the Egyptians did not have the technology to erect such structures. Scientists, though, have been able to trace the steps in the development of the pyramids.

The pyramid at Meidun, built around 2630 B.C., collapsed while under construction. Egyptian architects had not yet mastered the necessary building skills. The sides of the pyramid at Dahshur, erected some years later, change their angle about halfway up. This shows that the Egyptians were still working out the design problems. The Great Pyramid at Giza, which followed, is perfect. It shows that the Egyptians had taught themselves how to erect a pyramid, without any help from visiting astronauts.

Von Däniken is equally estranged from most archeologists on another issue, the origin of some unusual markings on the plain of Nazca in southern Peru. On this flat stretch of desert, about 9 by 40 miles (15 by 64 km), there are straight lines, some several miles long. There are also immense drawings of birds, fish, and other animals. All the markings were made by removing the surface rock to expose the sandy soil underneath.

This area, von Däniken concludes, was a landing field for the ancient astronauts. Then, after the astronauts left, the natives drew pictures of animals in an effort to lure them back.

Not so, say the scientists. Spaceships do not use ordinary landing fields. In addition, sandy soil is not good for landing any kind of craft. Finally, there is evidence that the markings form a very primitive calendar. One of the lines points to the place on the horizon where the sun sets on the shortest day of the year, and the others seem to mark off the days and months. The animal figures represent several of the constellations seen in the southern sky.

Scientists can explain in more acceptable terms the Biblical events that concerned Velikovsky and the objects from the past that concerned von Däniken. Velikovsky, von Däniken, and their followers take exception to this. Going against reason, they have led the scientific community to regard them as eccentric and misguided in their views.

Because of poor design, the early Meidun pyramid (top left) collapsed while it was being
built. The Dahshur pyramid (top right) shows that
the Egyptians were still learning how to con-
struct these monuments. Bottom: the lines and
figures on the desert plain of Nazca in Peru.

CHAPTER 5

DIZZY DABBLERS
DEAD ENDS
OF SCIENCE

There are people with scientific training who say:

• Magellan did not voyage around the world in 1519; he just read his compass incorrectly.
• Neil Armstrong's walk on the moon in 1969 and the photos of earth taken from space, like the one on the left, are fakes; they are only clever attempts to fool the public.
• The moon has a diameter of 32 miles (52 km), not 2,160 miles (3,476 km), as the astronomers insist; it is only 2,550 miles (4,104 km) away, not the 240,000 miles (386,232 km) that scientists say.
• The sun is only slightly larger than the moon and is a mere 3,240 miles (5,213 km) distant, not 93 million miles (150 million km) as claimed by astronomers.

The members of the International Flat Earth Society, with headquarters in Lancaster, California, still believe that the earth is flat, a giant pancake in space. This was the commonly held view in ancient times. Since then, though, there has been such overwhelming proof that the earth is a globe that everyone accepts this model—except the members of the society.

The members go on to say that the middle of the flat earth is the North Pole. The Antarctic, a tall, icy edge surrounding the earth, prevents anyone from falling off. Those who *think* that they have gone to the South Pole are merely poor navigators who made a big circle around the lip of the earth.

The Flat Earth followers cannot understand why anyone questions their conclusions on the size and distance of the moon and sun. They tell doubters to just look up; they can see for themselves how small and close these celestial objects really are!

Unusual ideas on the shape and composition of the earth are certainly not new. In 1692, Dr. Edmund Halley, the British Astronomer Royal who identified the comet that bears his name, wrote that the earth consists of a 500-mile (805-km) thick crust. Inside, Halley said, is another shell the size of Mars and another one the size of Venus. At the core is a solid mass the size of Mercury.

In the eighteenth century, the distinguished Swiss mathematician Leonhard Euler stated that the earth was hollow and had a sun on the inside. Pierre Bouer, a French mathematician, measured the force of gravity on various peaks in the Andes Mountains of South America. Finding less gravity than he expected, Bouer also concluded that the earth was hollow and, further, that the inside was inhabited.

But it was a self-taught astronomer and decorated veteran of the War of 1812, Captain John Cleves Symmes (1780–1829), who did the most for the hollow-earth theory. Symmes believed that the earth was made up of five concentric spheres, balls within balls, and that the North and South Poles, which came to be called "Symmes' Holes," were openings leading to the inside. When birds migrated they were heading toward the openings and the warm air and bright light that Symmes said came from inside the earth.

For ten years, Symmes petitioned the United States Congress for money to explore the Symmes' Holes. "We will find a warm and rich land, stocked with thrifty vegetables and animals, if not men." Although twenty-five Congressmen finally voted to finance an expedition, Symmes died before he had an opportunity to go.

[34]

Left: in ancient times, everyone believed the earth was flat, as this early drawing shows. Below: this old print shows someone falling into the middle of the hollow earth.

Others, though, carried on the struggle to win acceptance for the hollow-earth theory. One of the most successful of these was a self-styled medical doctor, Cyrus Reed Teed, born in 1839. Dr. Teed's theory was based on his reading of various passages in the Bible. Teed agreed with Symmes's theory, but he went beyond Symmes to say that *we* live inside the hollow earth. The stars and planets are also inside the sphere. It is only the thickness of the atmosphere that prevents us from seeing across to the other side!

Dr. Teed worked so hard to convince others of his belief that he neglected his medical practice. He came to be called the "crazy doctor." Eventually, his vision gave rise to a religious cult called the Koreshan. The movement continued to flourish for four years beyond Teed's death in 1908.

People have long dreamed of inventing a perpetual motion machine. This machine, once started, would continue running by itself forever without the need for any outside energy. And it would produce extra energy that could be used to do work, like pumping water or grinding corn.

Just as some people have found it hard to accept the solid globe of the earth, so others have refused to acknowledge that it is impossible to build a perpetual motion machine. Accounts of perpetual motion machines date back over 700 years. The machines themselves range from being very clever to being very strange. Some seemed to come close to working; some never worked at all. They show the full range of wild ideas that exist in the human imagination.

In 1874, an American, John Worrell Keely, announced he had built a perpetual motion machine, an engine that ran on water but did not use it up. With this machine, he claimed, he could fire bullets, tear metal cables, and bend iron bars.

By offering very convincing demonstrations of his machine, Keely was able to raise $1 million and open a laboratory in Philadelphia. His goals were to build a train that could go from Philadelphia to New York using only 1 quart (about 1 l) of water and a steamship that could cross the Atlantic on only 1 pint (.5 l).

For twenty years the investors waited for Keely to produce his first working engine. They even gave him additional funds from time to time to continue his research. But in 1898, Keely died—without having built his miracle engine.

On his death, two professors from the University of Pennsylvania were asked to examine Keely's laboratory. They were asked to try to find out why Keely had been able to demonstrate perpetual motion in the lab but never was able to build a working machine. They found the answer beneath the floorboards. Keely had hidden a compressed air pump that he had obviously used to power all of his perpetual motion machines!

Although the scientists seeking a perpetual motion machine refuse to believe it, it is almost surely impossible to build such a device. The reason is a basic law of nature: Energy can neither be created nor destroyed. In every machine there is a part that rubs or pushes against something. It requires energy to overcome this rubbing or pushing. Without an outside source of energy any machine will, sooner or later, run out of energy and come to a halt.

In 1859 Charles Darwin provided strong proof for the theory of evolution. This theory states that life on earth developed slowly over millions of years and changed from simple to more complex forms. Since Darwin there have been a number of scientists who have refused to accept evolution. These scientists have had to go to great lengths to fit the facts to their beliefs.

Philip Gosse (1810–1888), for example, was a British naturalist who said that God created man and the world as we know it in a single act of creation and that there was no such thing as evolution. The Bible, he held, was literally correct, and the world was created in exactly six days some 6,000 years ago.

But Gosse had trouble explaining fossils. These are the remains of creatures that lived in the past and that have been used by scientists to trace the evolution of various plants and animals. Gosse finally said that God created the fossils at the same time as he created man—to give the impression that the earth had existed for millions of years before humans appeared!

One of the most distinguished twentieth-century anti-evolutionists was Dr. Louis T. More, a professor of physics at the University of Cincinnati. In 1925, More published a book in which he wrote that the many kinds of living beings on earth were created in their present form, but in a series of separate acts of creation by God.

George McCready Price (1870–1963) was one of the best-known opponents of Darwin. He was a professor of geology at a number

Trofim Lysenko's ideas on plant breeding went against the accepted views of other scientists.

of American colleges. Price wrote more than twenty books in which he said that the Bible's description of creation is literally true. He explained the various layers of fossils that scientists have discovered by saying that they were all put in place during the Great Flood, the same flood in which Noah escaped in the Ark.

The Austrian biologist, Paul Kammerer, did experiments in evolution in the early part of the twentieth century. He claimed that his results showed that acquired characteristics could be inherited. In other words, a change in a parent can be passed on to the offspring. This was later disproved in a famous experiment in which the tails were cut off several generations of mice but the offspring were all born with normal tails.

On the basis of his research Kammerer was offered a professorship at the University of Moscow. Soon after he arrived, though, the authorities found that he had faked the results of his experiments. He denied everything, but to no avail. In desperation, Kammerer committed suicide.

The Kammerer episode did little to interfere with the rise to power in Russia of Trofim D. Lysenko, born in 1898. A plant breeder, Lysenko also advanced the idea that acquired characteristics could be inherited. He was very successful in convincing the Soviet authorities that his discoveries would improve agricultural production.

Lysenko first rose to fame after a 1929 experiment in which he exposed some winter wheat seeds to extreme cold. The purpose, he explained, was to "shatter their heredity." He then planted the seeds in the spring and, according to his account, produced a bumper crop. Here was proof, he said, that changes brought about in seeds by exposure to cold would bring about changes in plants grown from those seeds.

Farmers all over the country were told to adopt Lysenko's way of preparing seeds. Unfortunately it proved to be a disaster. The treated wheat did not grow well. The result was a severe shortage of wheat that lasted for several years until the practice was dropped. Later it was found that Lysenko had tampered with the figures in his original experiment.

Lysenko's position as a leader of organized science in the Soviet Union, however, remained secure. Few scientists had the courage to speak out against him. Those who did were denounced publicly, imprisoned, or sent into exile.

Over the following thirty years, Lysenko announced a number of major discoveries. Each one was heralded by the government, which insisted that all farmers were to follow the new procedure. To make spring wheat more hardy, for example, Lysenko advocated soaking the seeds and planting them while they were still swollen with water. The crop yield was very poor as a result.

One year the potato crop was ruined by a virus infection. Instead of fighting the virus, Lysenko told the farmers to change the planting time for potatoes to the summer. (Potatoes are usually planted in the winter or early spring.) Plant trees in clusters, too, he said, so that they could protect each other against their natural enemies. And get new and more powerful machinery to dig the earth to a depth of 39 inches (1 m) instead of the usual 8 inches (20 cm).

These ideas, too, proved to be failures—and rather expensive failures at that. Since there was no scientific basis for most of his theories, Lysenko was finally discredited, and he was dismissed by the government in 1964. Russia then began the job of catching up with thirty years of agricultural progress.

MAD SCIENTISTS

IN FICTION

CHAPTER 6

CRACKPOT CREATORS
ARTIFICIAL LIFE

To create life by artificial means is undoubtedly one of the most ambitious goals ever conceived of by the human mind. At the same time, it is a goal that has captured the imaginations of some of our maddest fictional scientists.

The first and best-known laboratory-made fictional creature was invented by Mary Shelley in the summer of 1816, while she was in Switzerland with her husband, Percy Bysshe Shelley, and Lord Byron, both poets. A popular topic of discussion among the three was the so-called "principle of life," a force that could bring inanimate objects to life.

The Shelleys and Lord Byron also spoke of the work of Luigi Galvani, who had discovered that electricity could cause the muscles of a dead frog's leg to twitch. All this led to speculation on the possibility of bringing a corpse to life by means of electricity.

After an evening of such talk, Mary had a dream that someone was kneeling beside a body he had pieced together from several corpses. Then, by means of a powerful force, the body was brought to life. It was this vision that Mary decided to develop in her novel, *Frankenstein.*

Victor Frankenstein, a university science student, starts a research project aimed at creating a living human being. For a whole year he collects body parts from morgues and graveyards. Day after day he toils at assembling them into a body. He becomes sick and feverish with exhaustion.

Finally, although Mary Shelley gives no details, Frankenstein succeeds in "discovering the cause of generation and life." She goes on to say how "on a dreary night of November [he lights the] spark of being into the lifeless thing." And then, "I saw the dull yellow eye of the creature open; it breathed hard, and a convulsive motion agitated its limbs."

Spurned by Frankenstein, the creature escapes and runs off into the forest. Although he is seeking only friendship, he is attacked by all those he meets. They are repelled by his size and ugly looks. Even a small boy reviles the monster. When it turns out that this little boy is Frankenstein's small brother, the monster strikes and kills the child. "I am malicious because I am miserable," he says.

The monster returns to the scientist. He demands that Frankenstein make a female creature to be his companion. "Make me happy, and I shall again be virtuous," the monster tells Frankenstein. Frankenstein begins work on a female, but before completing it he changes his mind. He fears that she, too, might turn to evil deeds. Together they might breed a race of monsters. So Frankenstein tears the body of the woman to pieces before it is finished.

This illustration from an early edition of the novel *Frankenstein* shows the scientist staring at the being he has just created.

The monster sets out to take revenge on Frankenstein. Among his most wicked deeds is the murder of Frankenstein's bride. Then the monster flees. Frankenstein follows the creature to the arctic wastelands. Before he reaches him, though, the scientist falls sick. Frankenstein admits on his deathbed that his studies were the work of a madman.

At the time Mary Shelley wrote *Frankenstein*, the world was turning away from alchemy. The new interest was electricity and its alleged magical powers. In fact, it is said that Shelley named the scientist Frankenstein after Benjamin Franklin, who was well known for his experiments with electricity.

Frankenstein's monster is truly a product of modern science. The "instruments of life" that Frankenstein assembles are more electrical than chemical. Although Mary Shelley was only nineteen when she wrote the book, and modern science was in its infancy, some feel that she foresaw the huge possibilities of modern science to generate both good and evil.

Mary Shelley's novel provided the inspiration for the most famous of all mad-scientist films, *Frankenstein,* released in 1931 and starring Colin Clive as Dr. Frankenstein, with Boris Karloff as the monster.

The film begins with Frankenstein and his misshapen assistant in a cemetery collecting parts of corpses that will be used to make the monster. The assistant later steals a preserved brain from a medical school. By accident, though, he takes the brain of an executed criminal.

An old mill serves as Frankenstein's laboratory. Inside it is a wonderland of electrical gadgets. Sparks fly, lights flash on and off, and large glass jars glow with eerie lights.

Frankenstein has assembled the body on the laboratory table. The heavily bandaged figure lies still, awaiting the flow of electricity that will give it the "spark of life." As a violent storm rages outside, Frankenstein and his helper turn cranks that slowly and dramatically raise the table and body to an opening in the top of the tower. The table reaches the top just as the storm is at the peak of its fury. Bolts of lightning crash down on the body.

After a few minutes, Frankenstein lowers the body. The storm slackens a bit. When the table is down, Frankenstein stares at the wrapped form. He sees the creature's hand begin to move.

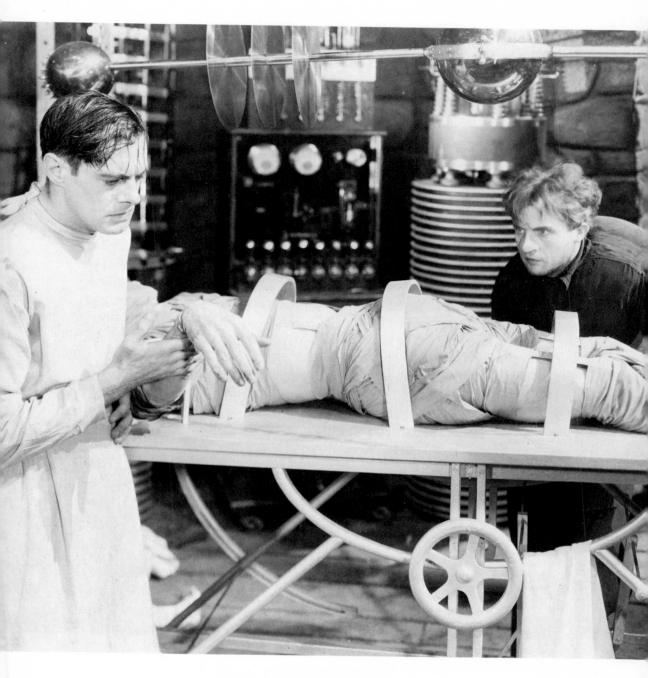

**The creature's hand begins to move.
Frankenstein has succeeded in
creating life in the laboratory.**

In *The Bride of Frankenstein,* Dr. Praetorius,
another mad scientist, works with Frankenstein
to create a mate for the monster.

Despite having a murderer's brain, the film monster, like the monster in the novel, at first seeks only friendship and love. But he, too, is met with hatred and cruelty. These injustices unleash his anger and murderous tendencies. The picture ends with both Frankenstein and his monster dying in a blazing windmill.

The immense success of the film led to a sequel, *The Bride of Frankenstein,* which was released in 1935. The inspiration for this second film came from the incident in the novel where Frankenstein starts to create a female mate for the monster. Although both Frankenstein and the monster seem to die at the end of the first film, in *The Bride of Frankenstein* it is shown that they have both survived.

Another mad scientist, Dr. Praetorius, is introduced in *The Bride of Frankenstein.* Praetorius shows Frankenstein his collection of tiny, perfectly shaped human creatures that he keeps in glass jars. The creatures are the result of twenty years of experimentation. "I grow my creatures like cultures. Grow them as nature does, from seed," Praetorius explains. He then suggests that Frankenstein and he cooperate to create a mate for the monster.

Together the two mad scientists sew up the parts needed for the female creature. The body lies in bandages on the lab table. On a stormy night, even more violent than the one in the original *Frankenstein,* the body is raised to the opening in the tower and the creature receives a surge of electricity from the flashes of lightning. As the body is lowered, the background music sounds soft wedding bells. Frankenstein feels for the pulse of the creature. She is indeed alive.

At this moment, the monster enters the laboratory. He reaches for his bandaged bride. "Friend?" he asks beseechingly. She answers with a loud scream of fright.

"She hate me. Like others," the monster says as a tear slowly rolls down his cheek. Then he goes berserk. He starts to wreck the lab, breaking and destroying everything in sight. No one is able to stop him. Suddenly Frankenstein cries out, "Don't pull that lever, you'll blow us all to atoms!"

Before pulling the lever, the monster utters the famous last line of the film, "We belong dead." The lab and everyone in it disappear in a gigantic explosion.

Many consider *The Bride of Frankenstein* a better film than its predecessor and truer to the novel on which both were based. It, too, proved a great success, and its characters were revived repeatedly to perform in still more sequels. To date, at least thirty Frankenstein films have been made!

One of the more interesting of these later films was *Frankenstein 1970.* The plot concerns a television crew that is using Frankenstein's laboratory, now equipped with the latest electronic equipment, to tape a horror story. Boris Karloff, who played the role of the monster in the original, here plays the role of the mad scientist.

The 1974 film, *Young Frankenstein,* may well be the last Frankenstein picture. In this hilarious take-off on the Frankenstein story, the doctor's grandson returns to the old castle and decides to make his own living creature. By introducing so many jokes and gags, and by poking fun at the most dramatic parts of the story, *Young Frankenstein* has made it very hard for anyone to take the tale seriously anymore.

Scream and Scream Again has become a sort of classic as a mad-scientist-creating-life story. This film, made in 1970, is far more horrifying and bloody than any of the Frankenstein films. It tells about the mad Dr. Browning, played by Vincent Price, who commits a series of murders to collect body parts and a supply of blood. His purpose, of course, is to create life in his laboratory. Browning constructs his creatures to look like ordinary people, but actually they are superhuman in their ability to win and hold positions of great political power. His hope is to create a whole race of these creatures so that he can take control of all the governments of the world.

As soon as Browning finishes a creature, he sends it out to kill another victim. In a particularly gruesome scene, one of Dr. Browning's supermen is caught. The police handcuff him to the front bumper of a car to await a patrol car. A little while later, they discover that the murderer has escaped—leaving his severed hand behind!

In a final twist of the plot, Dr. Browning turns out to be a laboratory-made person himself, and he dies by being dissolved in a bath of acid.

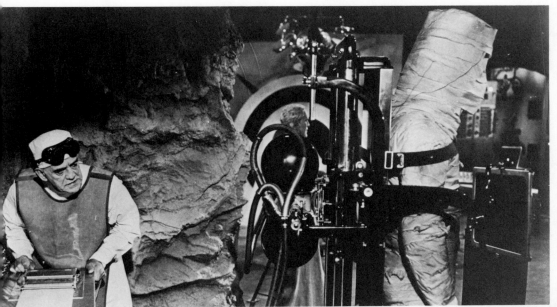

Above: *Frankenstein 1970* features Boris Karloff
as the mad scientist. **Below:** *Young Frankenstein*
is a comedy spoof of the original story.

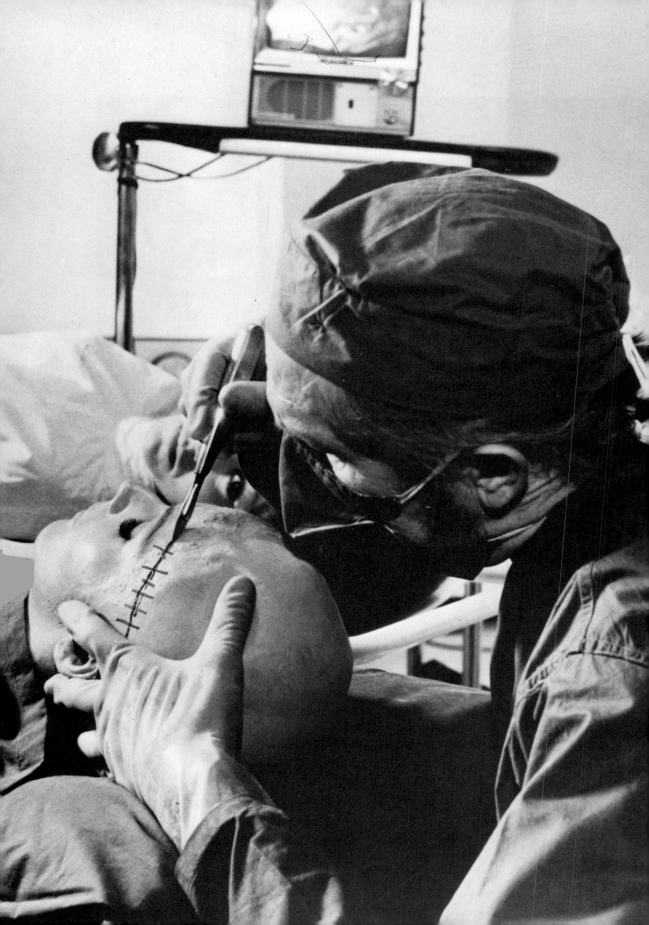

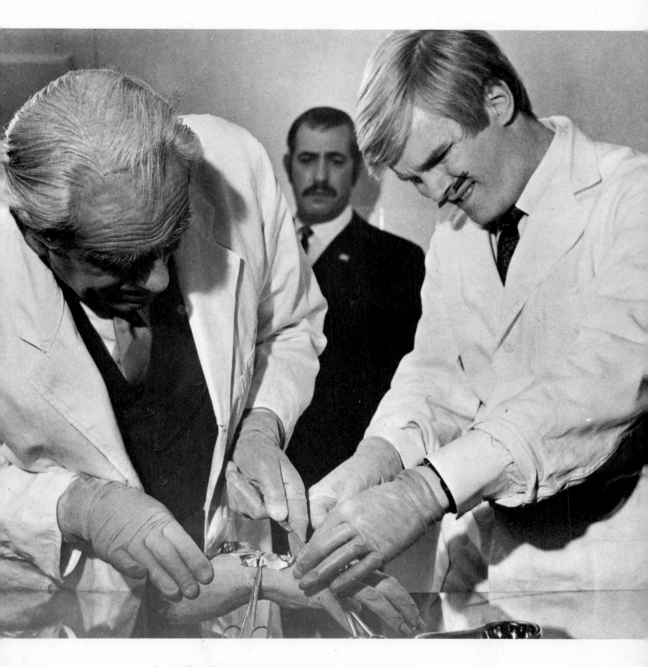

Left: Dr. Browning, in *Scream and Scream Again*, collects body parts to create artificial people in his laboratory. Above: two doctors examine a severed hand in this gruesome scene from *Scream and Scream Again*.

CHAPTER 7

EERIE EXPERIMENTERS
CONTROLLING
EVOLUTION

For some time now, real scientists have had a clear understanding of how evolution works, how living things change over millions of years. But this knowledge never stopped the mad scientists of fiction from conducting weird experiments in evolution.

The first fictional mad scientist to work in the field of evolution was Dr. Moreau in the 1896 novel by H. G. Wells, *The Island of Dr. Moreau*. Moreau is a prominent physiologist in nineteenth-century London. A reporter looking for a story gets a job as the doctor's lab assistant and writes an article about a horribly mutilated dog he discovers in the laboratory. The story creates a sensation, and Dr. Moreau is forced to leave England.

The ambitious doctor ends up on a tiny South Sea island, and it is here that we learn the true nature of his research. Moreau believes he can speed up evolution by turning wild animals into people. To prove his theory, he performs a number of cruel experiments on living humans and animals. These procedures take place in his laboratory, called the House of Pain. They involve grafting animal flesh and bones onto humans or attaching human body parts to animals.

There is little plan or organization to Moreau's research. He just joins parts of humans and parts of animals in an almost random way. The result is a number of tragic figures, Beast People they are called, who are neither human nor animal. Among them is M'ling, a cross between a dog and a man. Moreau also creates ape-men, leopard-men, and the strong workers on the island, the bull-men. Experiments with women produce swine-women, puma-women, and a wolf-woman. In operations that join parts of different animals together, Dr. Moreau creates the hyena-swine, the ape-goat, and the bear-bull. He keeps all the Beast People locked up or in chains.

In time the Beast People revolt. They break free and kill the mad Dr. Moreau. Then, gradually, they all lose their human qualities and become wild animals completely.

Of the three different films based on the original novel, the best known are the 1933 Paramount release, *The Island of Lost Souls,* and the 1977 American International version, *The Island of Dr. Moreau.* The earlier film is the better known of the two. Several additions were made to the story to adapt it for the screen.

A handsome young American is shipwrecked on Dr. Moreau's island. The doctor wants him to mate with Lota, a beautiful creature fashioned from a woman and a panther. Lota is the most successful of Dr. Moreau's creations. Moreau believes that if Lota and the American have a child, it would prove his theories and bring him the attention and recognition he thinks he deserves.

The climax of the film is the revolt staged by Moreau's victims. They drag the doctor off to the House of Pain to punish him for his cruelty. A fire breaks out, however, and everyone is killed except Lota and her American lover.

Edgar Allan Poe's "Murders in the Rue Morgue" is a detective story in which the murderer proves to be an ape. When the story was made into a film in 1932, a mad scientist, Dr. Mirakle, was added to the story and became the main character of the film. The role of Dr. Mirakle was played by Bela Lugosi, the master actor of Hollywood's horror films.

At the end of *The Island of Lost Souls,*
Dr. Moreau's victims drag him off to the House of Pain.

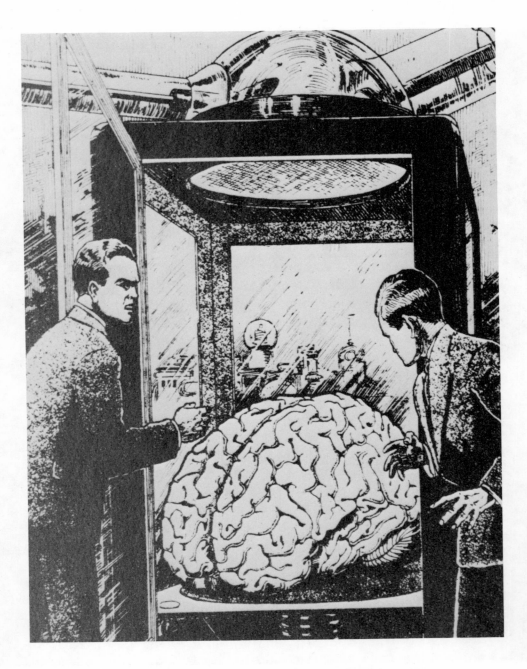

**The mad scientist in Edmond Hamilton's novel,
The Man Who Evolved, exposes himself to concentrated
cosmic rays and turns into a giant brain.**

Dr. Mirakle believes that humans evolved directly from apes and that the two are much closer and more alike than scientists believe. His experiments, done mostly on apes and women, are designed to prove his theory.

The doctor supports his research by running a sideshow in a circus. The main attraction of the sideshow is Erik, a large, fearsome gorilla. Whenever Dr. Mirakle sees a woman in the audience he would like to use in his research, he gives her a bracelet with tiny, tinkly bells on it. Then at night, Dr. Mirakle frees Erik. The ape traces the sound and brings the woman back to the lab for the experiments. The evil doctor, who makes Erik cooperate in his sadistic experiments, is finally strangled by the ape.

Edmond Hamilton tells about evolution and a mad scientist in his science fiction novel, *The Man Who Evolved* (1931). The scientist, aware that certain types of rays can influence evolutionary change, decides to expose himself to concentrated cosmic rays. He wants to see if he can actually bring about changes in himself.

First, he builds a collector to capture and store the cosmic rays that are always bombarding earth from outer space. Then he turns a beam of these rays on himself. His body, and his mind, too, begin to change. Finally, he is nothing more than a gigantic brain.

The scientist then decides to go one step further. He exposes himself to one last burst of cosmic rays. The result is horrifying. He dissolves into a blob of cells, not unlike the first living things on earth. The point that Hamilton appears to be making is that there may be a limit to evolution, and once humans reach that limit, evolution may reverse itself and start all over again.

Dr. Sigmund Walters is an expert in gland disorders in the 1943 film, *Captive Wild Woman*. Walters uses gland transplants and plastic surgery to try to bring about an evolutionary change of an ape into a human—with disastrous results.

Walters, played by John Carradine, visits a circus where he notices that Cheela, a large female orangutan, shows a great deal of affection for her trainer. He kidnaps the ape and tries to change her into a human being by giving her gland transplants. At one point, Walter's nurse threatens to expose the scientist. Dr. Walters kills the nurse and places her brain into the skull of the creature.

As a result of the operation, Cheela the ape becomes Paula Dupree, a beautiful young woman. Dr. Walters takes Paula to the circus. She is so good at calming excited animals that she is hired as an animal trainer. But when Paula sees the man she loves with another woman she becomes furious and reverts to being Cheela the ape. Dr. Walters, however, is able to change her back again into human form.

At the end of the film, Paula saves her lover from being killed by a lion. At the same time, though, she is transformed again into an ape. A policeman, unaware of who she is, shoots and kills her, effectively ending Dr. Walters' experiment.

CHAPTER 8

DEMENTED DEMONS
THE EVIL WITHIN

Most mad scientists in fiction are men who use science to serve their own evil purposes. Some start with good motives. But for one reason or another, they all end up doing cruel or horrible experiments or applying scientific knowledge to killing or controlling other people.

In his classic story, *The Strange Case of Dr. Jekyll and Mr. Hyde,* (1886), Robert Louis Stevenson expresses the idea that every person has an evil side to his or her nature. Dr. Henry Jekyll, a respected and reputable London physician, becomes aware of the wicked side of his personality. He gets the idea that he will become a better and more moral person if he can release this dark part of his being.

The doctor prepares a drug in his laboratory that unleashes the hidden aspect of his character. As soon as he takes the drug, the gentle Dr. Jekyll becomes the evil Mr. Edward Hyde. The fearful and brutal Hyde commits acts of great violence, including murder.

**Dr. Henry Jekyll is a respected London physician
who becomes aware of the evil side of his personality.
Under the influence of the drug, the gentle Dr. Jekyll
becomes the murderous Mr. Hyde.**

But he is never caught, because each time he escapes to the laboratory, takes an antidote, and changes back to Dr. Jekyll.

As time goes on, though, the Hyde part of the split personality grows stronger and stronger. Finally, Dr. Jekyll can no longer control his experiment. He is helpless to return to his true state. As the full horror of what is happening to him becomes clear, he takes his own life, leaving a letter of explanation for others to read.

Eleven years after Stevenson published his story, it was made into a stage play. In 1908 the first of some fifteen different film versions of the original tale was made. Three of the most outstanding, those of 1920, 1932, and 1941, are still shown.

The 1920 film starred John Barrymore, the great Broadway actor, in the double role of Jekyll and Hyde. One of the most remarkable features of this film was the way that Barrymore, without using makeup, was able to transform his appearance from the handsome, young Dr. Jekyll to the hideous, beastlike Mr. Hyde.

Most critics consider the 1932 version, with Fredric March in the title role, as the best of the Jekyll and Hyde films. March won an Academy Award for his performance, the only actor ever playing the part of a mad scientist to do so.

The last film, made in 1941, had Spencer Tracy playing both parts. By this time, Hollywood had developed so many tricks and illusions that the changes back and forth between Jekyll and Hyde were much more gradual and therefore not nearly as striking as they were in the earlier films.

The year 1932, which saw Fredric March play the role of Dr. Jekyll and Mr. Hyde, also saw two other films dealing with mad, evil scientists. *Dr. X* starred Lionel Atwill as Dr. Xavier, Director of the Academy of Surgical Research. The police are led to the academy by their investigation of a number of murders in which the bodies of the victims had been partially eaten.

To help the police solve the murders, Dr. Xavier sets up a bizarre experiment in which several people at the academy reenact the crimes. At the last minute, everyone realizes that the killer is about to strike again. He is Dr. Wells, one of the surgeons on the staff. Although Dr. Wells has only one arm, he wears an artificial limb made of synthetic flesh that he himself developed. But the synthetic flesh brings out the violent, hateful side of his nature,

**In the 1932 movie *Dr. X*, Dr. Xavier sets up a
bizarre experiment in which a murder is reenacted.**

turning him into a mad killer, just as Jekyll's drug turned him into the murderous Hyde.

In an exciting climax, Dr. Wells is shot and killed by the police. Before he dies, though, he shouts out that it was not Dr. Wells who was the murderer but someone else within his body.

Boris Karloff was the star in the other mad scientist film of 1932, *The Mask of Fu Manchu,* based on the novel by Sax Rohmer. Karloff plays the part of the sinister Dr. Fu Manchu, who is searching for Genghis Khan's sword and death mask. He plans to use them to incite Oriental people all over the world to join in a war against whites. In his ultramodern laboratory, Dr. Fu uses the most advanced equipment to torture his victims and force them to help him in his search. At the end, though, his electrical death-ray machine goes out of control, killing Dr. Fu and his followers.

H. G. Wells's novel, *The Invisible Man* (1897), furnished the plot for the highly successful film of the same name. It is the story of Jack Griffin, a research scientist who is studying a rare Indian drug called monocaine. When Griffin injects some monocaine into a dog, the animal turns completely white and then goes mad. When he injects some of the drug into his own arm, he finds that it makes him invisible.

Griffin is forced to wear a big, heavy coat, with gloves, hat, dark glasses, and bandages over his face in order to be seen when he goes out. Then he decides to go into hiding until he can find an antidote to the drug. But before long he realizes what great power he wields by being invisible. He sets out to gain control of the world by spreading terror and fear.

After several incidents of murder and robbery, including one dramatic scene in which he derails a train, the police are all searching for the Invisible Man. But since they cannot see him, they cannot catch him.

Eventually, however, he is caught and killed. As he dies, he gradually becomes visible again.

**Boris Karloff plays
the role of the
evil mad scientist in
*The Mask of Fu Manchu.***

**Left: Griffin works in his laboratory to find
an antidote to monocaine. Above: the police
and suspicious townspeople confront Griffin
in this scene from *The Invisible Man*.**

Dr. Anton Phibes, in the 1971 film, *The Abominable Dr. Phibes,* believes he is justified in the murders he commits. He is badly injured in an accident, and because of the poor medical care he receives, he is left with a horribly disfigured face. Later, when poor treatment by a team of nine doctors leads to his wife's death, Phibes determines to avenge himself on them. As an added dramatic touch, he decides to kill the doctors with plagues like those described in the Bible's Book of Exodus.

Thus, he kills the first doctor with bee stings. The second is bitten by poisonous bats. On and on he goes, until finally he fills his own body with embalming fluid and buries himself in a tcmb next to his wife.

**Dr. Phibes is left with
a horribly scarred and
disfigured face in the film,
*The Abominable Dr. Phibes.***

CHAPTER 9

MODERN MADMEN
SCIENCE FACT INTO SCIENCE FICTION

Most mad scientists in fiction are entirely products of their creators' imaginations. But there are some fictional mad scientists whose stories are based on real science and reflect the times in which they were written.

After World War I, for example, the science of prosthesis—providing artificial limbs for the human body—was born. Scientists were trying to create body parts that imitated, or even surpassed, limbs or bones lost through accident or disease. The 1935 film, *Mad Love,* grew out of this line of research.

Mad Love is about Dr. Gogol, played by Peter Lorre, who is known throughout Paris for his good work in treating physically disabled children and wounded soldiers. He loves Yvonne Orlac, an actress and the wife of pianist Stephen Orlac, but she spurns his love.

Both of Stephen's hands are badly mutilated in a train accident.

[73]

Yvonne asks Dr. Gogol to treat her husband, and Gogol hatches a scheme. He takes the hands of Rollo, a knife-throwing murderer who has just been beheaded, and grafts them onto the musician.

The hands of the murderer gradually take over the pianist's personality. Stephen flings knives whenever he is angry. Gogol takes advantage of this tendency to frame Stephen for his father's murder. Later, he adds to Stephen's confusion by pretending to be the ghost of Rollo.

In the climactic scene of the film, Gogol attempts to show his love to Yvonne. But she fights him off, and Gogol, in a fury, tries to strangle her, saying, "Every man kills the thing he loves." Though Stephen is able to see what is happening through a narrow slit in the locked door, he is unable to get inside. His only hope is to use his knife-throwing skill. Taking careful aim, he flings the weapon through the slit, killing Gogol and saving his wife.

Some real scientists were doing research on an artificial heart in the last years of this same decade. Accounts of their work inspired the 1939 film, *The Man They Could Not Hang.* Dr. Henryk Savaard, played by Boris Karloff, invents a mechanical heart in the hope of helping the sick and prolonging life. In order to test it, though, he convinces a young student to allow himself to be killed, so that the mechanical heart can be implanted in the boy's body.

The student's girlfriend learns what is happening and calls the police. When they arrive, they find Savaard in the middle of his experiment, with the boy lying dead on the table. Savaard is brought to trial for murder, found guilty, and hanged. His assistant, however, brings Savaard's body to the lab where he installs the artificial heart in it, bringing the doctor back to life.

Maddened by the fact that he was not allowed to finish his experiment, Savaard sets out to avenge himself on the jurors who sentenced him to death. At the end he destroys the artificial heart, taking its secret to the grave with him.

The science of physics took some great strides forward in the closing years of the nineteenth century. New elements such as radium were discovered. Radioactivity and the dangers of radioactive rays and particles were also found. And more and more uses for electricity were explored as the new science of electronics was born.

These advances furnished ideas for several mad scientist films and books. The 1936 film, *The Invisible Ray,* was one of the first motion pictures to deal with radium. *The Invisible Ray* stars the two greatest mad scientist actors, Boris Karloff, as the evil Dr. Janos Rukh, and Bela Lugosi, as the good Dr. Felix Benet.

The film opens in Dr. Rukh's laboratory and astronomical observatory on an eerie peak high in the Carpathian Mountains. Rukh has invented a combined telescope and television camera that can trace the paths of stars and planets far back into history. Using this instrument, he follows a giant meteor that came from beyond the Andromeda galaxy and crashed into the African jungle millions of years earlier.

With the help of Dr. Benet, Dr. Rukh organizes an expedition to find the meteor. When he locates it, Rukh discovers that the meteor contains the powerful element, Radium X. He believes that the rays from this substance can help humanity, and he plans to use them to cure blindness.

What he does not realize, though, is that he himself has been poisoned by the invisible rays. He begins to glow. He is able to shatter statues with a glance. His touch actually kills people.

Dr. Benet creates an antidote that controls the radiation, so long as Rukh takes some of the antidote every day. But the Radium X has disturbed Rukh's mind. He begins to imagine that everyone who was on the expedition is conspiring against him. Seeking revenge, he plans to kill each one.

Rukh's blind, elderly mother knows the cruel, vicious acts her son is planning. She is also aware that Rukh cannot live without the antidote. She dashes the last remaining dose from his hand just as he is about to drink it. As his body bursts into flame, Rukh jumps through the window and plummets to his death.

Dr. Thorkel is the evil mad scientist in the 1940 film, *Dr. Cyclops.* In his jungle laboratory, high in the mountains of Peru, he uses radium rays to try to shrink people to the size of dolls.

The mad doctor first tries the powerful rays out on a horse, who shrinks to the size of a dog. Then he entices a party of scientists to come to his laboratory and help him with his work. When they refuse to cooperate, he turns the ray gun on them, reducing them all to creatures 1 foot (.3 m) tall.

[75]

Left: the mad Dr. Rukh, on the left, explains the telescope with which he can look into the past. Above: when his mother smashes the bottle containing the antidote, Dr. Rukh bursts into flame and dies.

As the result of his experiment, the
scientists who come to visit Dr. Thorkel
are reduced in size to tiny creatures.

The tiny scientists escape from him and try to hide. They have many frightening adventures, including an attack on them by dogs and cats, who seem like giant beasts to the shrunken humans.

Dr. Thorkel pursues the scientists. He shoots one and tries to set fire to the others. Thinking they are all dead, he returns to his cabin and falls asleep. Three of the survivors creep in and smash his thick, heavy glasses, leaving him almost completely blind. Then they lead him to an open mine shaft, where he falls to his death.

Dr. Rigas, in the 1941 film, *Man-Made Monster,* wants to use electricity to create a race of superhumans, whom he would then be able to control. His first subject is a carnival performer, Dynamo Dan the Electrical Man, who is immune to electrical shock.

Dr. Rigas experiments on Dan. He sends increasing amounts of current through Dan's body. While the electrical charge does not harm Dan physically, it does rob him of his free will. A walking zombie, Dan kills a man who discovers his secret. Though he is sentenced to death in the electric chair, the shock does not bother him at all. Later he kills the warden and escapes from prison.

To help him conserve his electricity, Dr. Rigas fits Dan with a rubber suit. In a surprise move, Dan turns on the mad doctor as Rigas is about to send an electrical current through a girl's body. Dan frees the girl and carries her off into the night. But in the darkness he runs into a barbed wire fence, ripping his rubber suit. A great surge of electricity shoots through his body, and, as he dies, the girl escapes to safety.

The British-made film of 1956, *The Gamma People,* has one of the most interesting of all the mad scientist plots. Dr. Boronski, the ruler of the fictional European country of Gudavia, launches a drive to try to increase the brain power of Gudavia's citizens.

Boronski develops a machine that can send out a powerful beam of radioactive gamma rays. He hopes that the radiation will produce a nation of geniuses. For his first experiments, he chooses as his unwilling victims a number of children and aged men and women.

The results are horrible. Some die immediately. Others are struck dumb, unable to speak. Only a very few become brighter after the treatment. But everyone who does survive becomes a zombie, one of the living dead, without any willpower or emotion.

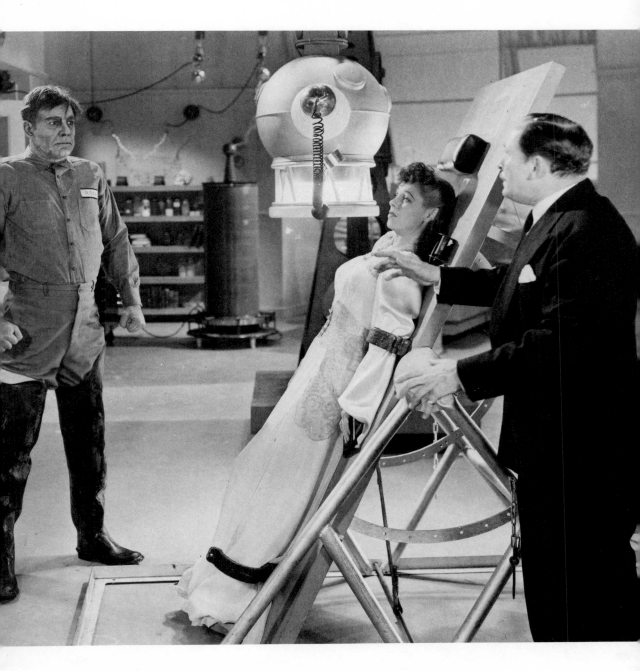

Left: Dr. Rigas fits Dan with a rubber suit so that his electricity will not leak out. Above: Dan attacks Dr. Rigas when he sees the mad scientist about to perform his experiments on a girl.

In *The Gamma People,* powerful
gamma rays are used to try
to improve people's brain power.

Despite his many failures, Dr. Boronski continues beaming the gamma rays on more and more Gudavians. Finally, there is an uprising. The citizens march to the laboratory and burn it down. Boronski, a symbol perhaps of dictators who would use modern science to control or destroy people, is annihilated.

We can be certain that science in the future will continue to venture into many new and as yet unexplored realms. Thus, we can be just as certain that there will be many more mad scientists of fact and fiction to come—involved in ever more imaginative and fantastic experiments.

SUGGESTED READING

Däniken, Erich von. *Chariots of the Gods?* New York: Putnam, 1974.

Francesco, Grete de. *The Power of the Charlatan.* New Haven: Yale University Press, 1939.

Gardner, Martin. *Fads and Fallacies in the Name of Science.* New York: Dover Press, 1957.

Goldsmith, Donald, ed. *Scientists Confront Velikovsky.* Ithaca, New York: Cornell University Press, 1977.

Holbrook, Stewart. *The Golden Age of Quackery.* New York: Macmillan, 1959.

Lasagna, Louis. *Doctor's Dilemmas.* New York: Arno Press, 1962.

Manchel, Frank. *An Album of Great Science Fiction Films.* New York: Franklin Watts, 1976.

Rottensteiner, Frank. *The Science Fiction Book.* New York: Seabury, 1975.

Shelley, Mary. *Frankenstein.* London: J. M. Dent, 1921; New York: Dell, 1964.

Story, Ronald. *The Space-Gods Revealed.* New York: Harper & Row, 1976.

Velikovsky, Immanuel. *Worlds in Collision.* New York: Doubleday, 1950.

Young, James Harvey. *Medical Messiahs.* Princeton, New Jersey: Princeton University Press, 1967.

INDEX